WINDSHOOK

by
MARY GALLAGHER

★

★

DRAMATISTS
PLAY SERVICE
INC.

WINDSHOOK was commissioned and produced in 1991 by
The Young Conservatory (Craig Slaight, Director) of the
American Conservatory Theater (Edward Hastings, Artistic Director).

The Play was revised and remounted in 1996 by
ACT (Carey Perloff, Artistic Director).

BIOGRAPHY

Mary Gallagher's plays, including FATHER DREAMS, LITTLE BIRD, CHOCOLATE CAKE, BUDDIES, DOG EAT DOG, LOVE MINUS, HOW TO SAY GOODBYE, ¿DE DONDE? and WINDSHOOK, have been published by Dramatists Play Service and produced at such theatres as the American Conservatory Theater, Actors Theatre of Louisville, Hartford Stage Company, Stage Left, the Main Street Theater and the Cincinnati Playhouse; in New York City at the Vineyard Theatre, the American Place Theatre, the Ensemble Studio Theatre and the New York Shakespeare Festival; and in many other countries.

Grants and fellowships: The Guggenheim Foundation, The Rockefeller Foundation, the NEA (two fellowships), The New York Foundation for the Arts. Prizes: The Susan Smith Blackburn Prize, 1986; The Rosenthal New Play Prize, 1989. Most recently: a 1997-98 NEA/TCG Residency Grant to develop a new mask theatre piece at Capital Repertory Company in Albany, New York, in collaboration with Gallagher's company, GYPSY, and Shelly Wyant's company, MaskWork Unlimited.

Screenplays include *Nobody's Child* (CBS, 1986), co-written by Ara Watson and directed by Lee Grant (Writers Guild Award, Luminas Award from Women in Film); *Bonds of Love,* starring Treat Williams (CBS, 1993), Best TV Movie of the Year at The Banff International Television Festival; features for MGM and Paramount, and TV movies for CBS, HBO, NBC, Lifetime and Showtime. *The Passion of Ayn Rand,* (1998), starring Helen Mirren and Peter Fonda, airs on Showtime, with European theatrical distribution. Gallagher is currently developing an independent film, *Hard-Headed Women,* set in New York's Hudson Valley, which she will produce and direct.

Gallagher is an alumna and board member of New Dramatists and a member of Actors & Writers in Ulster county, NY.

For Craig Slaight

ACKNOWLEDGMENT

My love and thanks to Craig Slaight, Director of the Young Conservatory and the New Plays Program at ACT, and to Edward Hastings and Carey Perloff, past and present Artistic Directors of ACT, for their faith in the play and commitment to my work.

Over the period of rewriting the play, I did a number of readings at New Dramatists in New York City. As always, my love and thanks to New Dramatists, putting faith in playwrights since 1949.

NOTE

The play began with an old folk song, one of the Child Ballads, called "The Mill o' Tifty's Annie." But as I wrote it, the story in the play took a different path from the story in the song. The melody of the song is sung by Ruby in the last scene of the play.

THE MASKS

WINDSHOOK was originally commissioned to be played by high school-age conservatory students. I decided that the young people were telling the story to the audience and they would put on character masks to play the adults — MOM, DAD and BROOKS — whom they saw as the powerful mythic figures who controlled their lives. So DARLENE put on a MOM mask to become MOM, and took it off again to become DARLENE again. The actors who played LANCE and DYLAN took turns playing DAD, depending on who else was in the scene with DAD.

I found that this works very well with a cast of young people. But when there are adult actors cast as the adults, the play becomes more "real" and the relationships more complex. Masks, which convey a heightened sense of reality, are no longer appropriate.

PLACE and TIME

The language of the play is that of the old families in the Catskills Mountains, only two hours' drive from New York City. This language is as deeply-rooted and specific as the language of the African-American inner city. The people who speak it have learned to speak differently at school. But among their own, or when they're making a point, they revert to it.

The time is the present, in summer and fall. Scenes happen in and out of doors in various locations, with few set pieces or props.

The play has no intermission and runs about an hour and forty minutes.

WINDSHOOK was commissioned by the Young Conservatory of the American Conservatory Theatre (Edward Hastings, Artistic Director) in San Francisco, California, where it received two workshop productions. The first production in 1991 featured students from the Young Conservatory. It was directed by Craig Slaight; the assistant director was Svetlana Litvinenko; the musical direction was by Maureen McKibben. The cast was as follows:

DARLENE/MOM .... Tyson Sheedy
RUBY .... Rainbow Rachel Underhill
DYLAN/DAD .... Andrew Irons
RAFE .... Devon Angus
JULIE .... Shona Mitchell
JACKIE/BROOKS .... Pavlos Politopoulos
LANCE/DAD .... Jon Lucchese

In the production, DAD, MOM and BROOKS were played by the same young actors playing the younger roles, who put on masks to assume the personalities of the adults.

The second production at ACT (Carey Perloff, Artistic Director) in 1996, featured professional actors from the ACT Company as well as students in the Adult Training Program and the Young Conservatory. A great deal of rewriting was done and the mask convention was dropped. There was no doubling. The cast was as follows:

DARLENE .... Chelsea Peretti
MOM .... Christianna Hauber
RUBY .... Katherine Foster
DYLAN .... Kevin Crook
RAFE .... Robert Oliver
JULIE .... Marcelle Rice
LANCE .... Michael Smith
DAD .... Warren David Keith
BROOKS .... Michael Fitzpatrick

CHARACTERS

DARLENE — 17. Ruby's friend. A good-natured fatalist. Married to Dale, a loser, and mother of a toddler, Ashley. Neither of these are seen.

CEELIE CARROLL (MOM) — 40s. A faded beauty, living with disillusionment. But she has a hidden energy, a secret dream.

RUBY CARROLL — 17. The prettiest girl in town, and the stubbornest. Her goal is to get out and keep on going.

DYLAN — 25. A drifter, till he finds a home. Lives on his charm, but he's wearing out.

RAFE — 20. As idealistic and stubborn as death.

JULIE — 20. Loves Rafe desperately, but is determined to have a different life.

LANCE — 20. Rafe's friend and Ruby's sometime boyfriend. Wildly-driven, frustrated. A talented dirt track racer.

MARLIN CARROLL (DAD) — 40s. Bright, charming, trapped, angry. A drunk, who still has control most of the time.

EVAN BROOKS — 30. The man with the money who changes everything without thinking of the consequences. Smart, charming, cold.

WINDSHOOK

Lights up on Darlene. To the audience.

DARLENE. After it happened, I just couldn't even go over to their house or nothing, not for weeks. I wouldn't even walk past it when I was wheeling Ashley, I'd go around by the back road past the old fire house. It's way out of the way, and we was having heavy rains, that back road was awash, just about ... but I just felt so bad.... But when I did go see her mom, finally, go by just to see did they need anything or what ... her mom said the saddest thing to me. She said, "I was the one who started it all up, Darlene. I seen him on the road, first day he was in town here, and I pointed him out to her. That's where it all begun." *(Lights up on Mom, in old gardening clothes. Her hands are grimy with dirt. She carries a trowel, stands U., gazing out toward the audience. Ruby enters behind her, in jeans and dirt-caked garden gloves, her hair raked back.)*

RUBY. Mom, you want me to spray the tomatoes too?

MOM. 'Course I do, wadaya think? Ruby, look at this boy that's passing. *(Dylan, with a backpack and a bedroll, enters D., strolling down the road, looking with interest and pleasure at the countryside.)* Don't he look like Dirk, who used to be on my soap?

RUBY. *(Looks; impressed, but not showing it.)* Don't look like much to me.

MOM. Choosy, ain't ya?... You don't know him?

RUBY. No. *(Dylan stops, dumps his pack and sits.)*

MOM. What's he doing out so far from town? — Oh, look, he's sitting down there by the creek — go on and wander by.

RUBY. *(Laughs.)* Get out!

MOM. Go on! He's cute!

RUBY. He'd know why I was doing it.

MOM. Well, ain't that terrible, for him to know.

RUBY. You go and wander by.

MOM. I'll tell you, if I was your age, I'd be after him.
RUBY. If he's around, I'll meet him soon enough.
MOM. Must be nice to be so cocky. *(Beat; all three women stare at Dylan. Then:)*
DARLENE. *(To the audience.)* That's where it all begun. *(Cross-fade as Darlene, Mom, Ruby and Dylan exit. Rafe enters. He speaks to the audience.)*
RAFE. I knew what I wanted. Since I was a little kid, I always had that dream. But my dad always said, "You can't eat bread you haven't earned." And ain't no way he'd ever go beyond that, not for me. So I had to earn it, had to show what I could do. Now how it is around here, you get oughta high school and there's only two places to go — the army or the prison. And working at the prison, that's good security. Them guards, they got their pensions in their minds first day they walk inside them gates. How I see it, they're lifers, worse'n cons are. I wanted more than that.... So I went for the army. Give it two years. If I liked it, I could save my money up. I could make a plan. *(Julie enters, wearing a yellow bow corsage and carrying a small yellow bow. She goes to Rafe, smiling, starts to pin the ribbon on him. To Julie, flatly.)* But the army didn't work for me. *(Very disappointed, Julie pins the ribbon on him anyway, then turns away, but stays near Rafe. The others enter: Ruby, with a cheap folding lawn chair which she places at C.; Dad, in jeans and a worn feed cap, with a six-pack of cheap beer; Lance, Rafe's friend and Ruby's sometime boyfriend; Mom, with a yellow bow corsage and a can of Coke, which she gives to Rafe. As the talk continues, Dad hands out beers to everyone but Rafe and then sits in the lawn chair. This is the lawn outside the Carroll house, and Rafe's coming home party. Ruby goes back offstage.)*
DAD. Hell, no. You work for the army. That's how *we* did it.
RAFE. I done it too. But I ain't signing up again.
MOM. You'd have a real good life in there. They help their own.
RAFE. That ain't all they do. You make a mistake and three guys rub your nose in it, like you're a dog that shit indoors.
LANCE. But what about the action, man? Did you kick some ass?

RAFE. Hell, no. We just sat and sweated. Or drilled and sweated and passed out. One guy in our outfit died 'cause he was drilling in his gas mask and protective suit, got too hot in there and panicked, had a heart attack.

MOM. But still, you boys went over there and you were ready. People appreciate that.

RAFE. Oh, yeah. Before we even got there, we had packages from strangers waiting for us to come. Boxes full of cookies and candy bars and lollipops, all melted down and beat to shit. And razor blades and toilet paper, like the army hadn't thought of stuff like that. And little gift-type stuff, Pocahontas key chains and Rush Limbaugh coffee mugs. And stuff they made, little knitted stuff … and all these letters from strangers, thanking us and praising us.…

DAD. When we was in Vietnam, we didn't get no letters. Nobody gave a damn.

RAFE. The worst part was just sitting. You go over there all rared up to show what you can do … and then you gotta sit on it.…

DAD. Yeah, you do. Like hunting. Main thing you gotta do is wait. I taught you that.

RAFE. You did. But waiting for the deer … out in the woods, all by yourself … it ain't the same as waiting with a thousand other guys. We took it out on each other some.

DAD. Sure you did. It's human. Sure.

RAFE. Then come to find out, we was going home. And we hadn't done nothing.

DAD. Well, I'll just say one thing and then I'll shut up. When we was in Vietnam, we knew why we was there and we knew what to do about it. And when we come home, we didn't sit around and cry-baby.

RAFE. … I ain't saying nothing against having a job to do.

DAD. Oh, well, good, that eases my mind. Where's that girl got to? *(Dad drinks his beer as Ruby enters with an open fifth of whiskey and a shot glass, comes to Dad.)*

MOM. *(To Rafe.)* Did you see all them little yellow bows along the fence? Julie and me did that. Took the best part of the afternoon.

RAFE. Looks nice, Mom.

DAD. *(Hits Ruby on the butt.)* Just pour that out for your old man. *(Ruby pours the shot and Dad takes it as Mom says to Rafe:)*

MOM. Julie come around to see me quite a bit while you was gone. She helped me out more than your sister. With the garden and the farmstand too.

DAD. *(A toast.)* Here's hoping all you good people live forever and I sit right beside ya. *(They all drink. Dad slaps his knee.)* Come on, Rube, sit with your old man once before you get too big.

RUBY. *(Sits on his lap.)* I'm too big already.

DAD. Oh, you ain't too big to spank.

LANCE. I'll spank her for you. *(Ruby ignores this.)*

DAD. I wouldn't put money on ya. *(Laughs, slaps Lance's back. To Ruby.)* Don't be so stingy with that bottle, Rube. *(Ruby pours him a shot.)*

LANCE. *(To Rafe.)* Hey, you want to go up to hunting camp on Sunday, shoot a mess of turkeys? I been cleaning house up there.

RAFE. *(Looks at Julie.)* Maybe. Hafta see. *(Dad gives Lance the shot. Lance drains it.)*

JULIE. *(To Rafe.)* My stepdad says they need people up to the prison.

RAFE. You know I ain't doing that.

DAD. *(To Lance.)* How's that now? Is that smooth?

JULIE. It ain't like you know the prisoners. They're all from the city. My stepdad says they're animals, some of 'em.

RAFE. They're men. And keeping other men locked up — I can't see my way to living my whole life like that.

JULIE. … Well, what *are* you gonna do?

RUBY. *(Takes the shot glass from Lance.)* My turn.

DAD. Listen to this, now … you will, will ya?

RUBY. Can I?

DAD. *(Proud of her.)* Aw hell, just don't say who give it to ya. *(Ruby holds the glass as Dad pours.)*

MOM. Marlin, she's too young for that. *(Dad and Ruby ignore her. Feeling the old wound of her exclusion, Mom watches.)*

RAFE. *(To Julie.)* What you been doing since I left?

JULIE. *(Letting him wonder.)* Not too much.
RAFE. How much is too much? *(Julie has to smile. Rafe smiles back: contact.)*
DAD. Watch this here, now. *(Everyone looks as Ruby nonchalantly drains the shot. Dad and Lance laugh.)* Now where d'ya think she gets that from?
MOM. And where's it gonna take her?
DAD. *(Gives Mom a cool glance, then:)* Yes, dear. *(To the others.)* My uncle Percy always told me, "Only two words a married man's gotta know — 'Yes, dear.' Keep saying 'em, you'll be all right."
RAFE. Uncle Percy had three wives. Kept leaving 'em. Has seven kids in three states and he never sees 'em. *(Brief pause.)*
RUBY. He musta kept saying, 'Yes, dear,' right up till he left. *(Dad laughs. Relieved laughter from all but Rafe — he's partly relieved, partly disappointed. Dad abruptly shoves Ruby off his knee. Indicating Rafe.)*
DAD. This one's left the army. Guess he's got a better idea how to make a living around here than the rest of us.
RAFE. No. But I know what I want.
MOM. You hear that, Ruby? Somebody around here knows. Ruby don't know *what* she wants, she just knows she ain't got it.
RUBY. *(Coolly.)* I'll know when I see it.
DAD. That's my girl.
RAFE. *(Plowing on.)* And now I got a plan.
DAD. Holy Jesus, Rafe, how'd I know it was you if you didn't have a plan? *(Laughter, sympathetic to Rafe but giving Dad what he wants.)*
RAFE. I want to get Granddad's farm going again. I thought it through this time. I got a little money saved, and I'm a veteran, I can get a loan and give you a down payment on the land and the old farmhouse — and I'm gonna buy a team of draft horses and use 'em to farm, and do farmwork for other folks, haul timber and plow and do their haying —
DAD. We work with machines around here —
RAFE. Week ends and summers, I'll give hay rides, and teach kids about the old times. And I'll do odd jobs too, work up

to the lumber yard, deliver stuff, whatever needs doing to bring a little money in —

DAD. Aw hell, why don't you make barrel hoops and sell 'em from a wagon? — that's the way you're talking.

RAFE. It ain't just me — you oughta read *The Small Farmer's Journal.* There are folks all over the country who've gone back to farming the old way —

DAD. Yeah, and they all got their heads up their asses. They think chickens are cute, 'cause they never had to get to know no chickens, and find out they're the dumbest, meanest critters out in nature. There ain't one of them fools that grew up on a farm like I did, where you had to get up every goddamn morning of your life before it was even light, to milk them goddamn cows — and if I overslept, my dad just come and threw me out of bed, and he was right to do it — 'cause winter, summer, Sundays, Christmas, it wasn't no different, it was the same chores to be done. And you had more chores *off* the farm — 'cause even if your whole family worked till your guts ached, you couldn't make your ends meet unless you had a couple of you working off the farm. You grow up on a farm, you got no *ro*-mance about farming. You shoulda stuck it out in the army, boy.

RAFE. Sell me the farm.

DAD. I told you to quit thinking of that years ago.

JULIE. *(Defiantly speaking up.)* He sold it off, Rafe. *(Silence. Rafe looks at his father, who won't look at him. Dad takes another shot.)*

RAFE. You sold off Granddad's farm while I was in the army?

JULIE. The house too. All of it.

DAD. *(To Julie.)* When did you join this family? *(To Rafe.)* I don't answer to you, boy. But I'll tell you this — all my life, I never had two nickels to rub together, no more'n my dad did, till I give up on farming. When I went to work for the propane company, that's when we started paying bills regular around here. Aw hell, ain't nobody even offered to farm that land in twenty years —

RAFE. I offered! You knew I always wanted it —

DAD. Ruby, talk some sense into your brother —

RAFE. Who'd you sell it to? *(Dad makes a disgusted gesture, starts to exit with the whiskey bottle.) Who was it?*

DAD. I'm going to bed. Some of us gotta work tomorrow. *(He exits. Rafe looks at Mom. She's helpless, torn.)*

RAFE. All my life....

JULIE. I know.

MOM. I know. But your dad ... he sees it different....

RAFE. You coulda talked to him —

MOM. I talked to him —

RAFE. You coulda written me about it —

MOM. It wouldn'ta helped none. *(Beat.)* Rafe ... that old-style farming, I always liked your idea of that. But when it comes to push and shove....

LANCE. Yeah, pretty tough row to hoe, Rafe —

RAFE. Nobody believed me.

JULIE. I believed you. *(Under his gaze, she weakens.)* I mean ... I knew you always really wanted it....

RAFE. Did you think I could *do* it?

JULIE. *(Weaker.)* ... If your dad woulda let you. *(Rafe turns away. Mom gives up, exits, leaving Rafe with Julie, Ruby and Lance.)*

RUBY. It's a guy from the city. Evan Brooks, his name is. Not too old either — maybe thirty. Kinda good-looking, in a way.

LANCE. Oh, yeah? *(Lance tries to drop an arm on Ruby's shoulder. She shrugs it off, goes on.)*

RUBY. I only seen him twice, he hardly ever comes up here. Don't know why he bought it. *(Beat.)* You gonna do something?

RAFE. I ain't gonna let it go.

RUBY. You better be careful, Rafe.

RAFE. You against me too?

RUBY. No, I don't care. But I'm just saying.... Dad could still hurt you if he wanted to —

RAFE. Not no more, he can't. *(Crossfade as they exit, Rafe in one direction, the others in another. Mom reenters, stands by the empty lawn chair, addresses the audience.)*

MOM. He talks like he hates farming, but you notice we still got the biggest garden on the road, with the farmstand out front, where we sell off what we don't eat or put up for the winter. The garden and the stand, that's my work, mostly — and Ruby, when I can catch ahold of her — but he acts like he hates all that. Every fall he says, "Aw, hell, let's not even plow up the field next year." But then come spring, he says, "Aw, hell, might's well put something in the ground." See, he can change his mind. If that Brooks from the city hadn't made his offer when he did, right after the tax bill come ... or if Marlin hadn't heard about the Harrises up in the vly* selling off their pasture land for fifty thousand dollars.... *(Brief pause.)*

But see, Rafe wanted him to keep the land for *Rafe* ... to have that be his reason. And he never woulda done that. He don't see life that way. Life is hard. Mostly you don't get what you want. But you take it and you keep your mouth shut and you do the best you can. Mostly he's been a good husband to me. And when he ain't ... mostly I don't hold them times against him. *(Hesitates, then:)*

But one time comes back up on me. I was sick, and the kids was sick, and it was hard winter. Marlin was out there following the county snowplows fourteen hours a day, trying to get the propane up to the folks who needed it, and coming home when he could and taking care of us. He didn't say nothing about it, that ain't his way. But one night when he finally laid down to sleep, the cat was sick right there under our bed. And Marlin, he got right up and cleaned up the cat-sick, and then he got dressed again. He took that cat, Alice her name was, and he drove off with her into the snow. When he come back, he didn't have no cat. *(Brief pause.)*

I didn't say nothing ... I could see how he come to do it ... but she was *my* cat. *(Beat.)* If she'da been Rafe's cat, it woulda been the same. Now, Ruby's cat, I don't believe he woulda done that way. *(Crossfade. Dylan enters, shirt off, pushing a wheelbarrow of fireplace wood. Mom watches him for a moment; drops her gaze to Dad's chair. She folds the chair and takes it as she exits. Ruby enters with a big shoulder bag, walking along the road D. of Dylan. The farmhouse would be U.; the meadow is out in the audience. Ruby keeps sauntering till indicated. Dylan sees her.)*

* "Vly" (rhymes with fly) is an old usage for "valley."

DYLAN. Hey.
RUBY. *(Glances.)* Hey.
DYLAN. Hey, hold on a minute.
RUBY. Why?
DYLAN. Why not?
RUBY. Gotta go to work.
DYLAN. Where?
RUBY. *(Smiling.)* Why?
DYLAN. *(Smiling.)* Why not? *(Ruby has passed him. Now she turns, whisks a McDonald's cap out of her bag, puts it on her head, walking backward.)* McDonald's? That's way out in Lindaville.
RUBY. I know it is. I gotta catch my ride.
DYLAN. I've got a truck, I'll take you. *(Ruby stops walking at last, considers this.)*
RUBY. You're not from around here.
DYLAN. Nope. Caretaking this place for the guy who owns it. He can vouch for me.
RUBY. He ain't around much.
DYLAN. *(Grins.)* No, it works out great. *(Ruby smiles back, but still considers. Dylan continues, low-key, charming.)* Beautiful land, isn't it? Especially this meadow across the road. You just picture horses in it. And this old house is pretty beat-up, but it's got style. I'll be sorry if he tears it down.
RUBY. *(Thrown by that idea.)* ... My granddad was born in it.
DYLAN. *(Even more intrigued.)* ... I'll go get the truck. *(Ruby watches him exit. Crossfade as Darlene enters with a grocery bag. She and Ruby take their McDonald's uniforms out of their bags and put them on as they talk. They're in the restroom.)*
DARLENE. Where'd you go last night? I thought you was coming out to the dirt track.
RUBY. Didn't feel like it.
DARLENE. Lance was looking for you. He looked good too, got his ear pierced in three places! Had little gold rings in, he looked so cool.
RUBY. *(Amused.)* That ain't gonna go over too good at the lumber yard.
DARLENE. Lisa was hanging on him, I'm serious. He won all his races too.

RUBY. *(Dismissive gesture like her father's.)* Aw hell, he always wins the quarter-mile, since he was twelve or something. Why don't he move up to the half-mile and go for it?
DARLENE. Why do you give him such a bad time? I wish Dale ever treated me half as nice as Lance treats you.
RUBY. I wouldn't take the shit you take from Dale, Darlene. And you don't have to either.
DARLENE. Well ... I got Ashley to think of now....
RUBY. You always took shit from him.
DARLENE. ... He don't mean it....
RUBY. What *does* he mean?
DARLENE. He don't mean nothing. You know Dale. He don't think that much.
RUBY. One of these days, he's gonna run you down in the V.I.P Lounge parking lot in that stupid high-wheeler he went and bought.
DARLENE. Well, see there, aren't you lucky, how nice Lance is to you? Lance'd do anything for you, if you'd just not spit on him.
RUBY. He likes it when I spit on him.
DARLENE. Do you want Lance or not? *(Beat; Ruby starts playing with Darlene's hair, twisting it around various ways as they look into an invisible mirror. Darlene lights a cigarette.)*
RUBY. You ever read the wedding announcements in the *Banner?*
DARLENE. You know we don't take a paper regular —
RUBY. *(Affectionate.)* Yeah, you only read the *Star.*
DARLENE. Hey, when I buy the *Star,* you read the whole thing —
RUBY. Yeah, but you believe it.
DARLENE. Well, it's right there in black and white, why wouldn't it be true?
RUBY. Darlene....
DARLENE. Well, I spose you don't believe the wedding announcements either.
RUBY. I believe 'em. That's what's wrong with 'em. "The bride is a medical receptionist. The bridegroom is a shipping clerk at Sears. After a honeymoon in Florida, they are living

in Lindaville."

DARLENE. I wish Dale was a shipping clerk at Sears.

RUBY. "The bridegroom is a plumber's assistant. The bride is a clerk at the Crawley Laundromat. After a honeymoon in the Poconos, they are living in Crawley."

DARLENE. I bet I'll never in my whole life see the Poconos.

RUBY. You're missing the point, Darlene! Is that all they're gonna get? Prob'ly get pregnant on their stupid boring honeymoon, if they ain't already, and forever after they'll be "living in Crawley"! Don't that depress you?

DARLENE. Yeah, they depress me 'cause they're so much better off than me.

RUBY. I give up.

DARLENE. You're just spoiled is all. *(Ruby looks at her in the mirror. Darlene nods wisely. Ruby slowly smiles.)*

RUBY. ... Maybe.

DARLENE. Are you seeing somebody besides Lance?

RUBY. I ain't seeing Lance.

DARLENE. *Are* you? *(Beat; Ruby drops Darlene's hair, picks up her shoulder bag. Darlene ponytails her hair.)*

RUBY. ... I don't know what I'm doing yet....

DARLENE. Well, you seem all wired up to *me.*

RUBY. That's 'cause everyone around here is dead, and I'm alive. *(Ruby exits with her bag. Darlene grabs her bag and follows Ruby out. Crossfade to Rafe at a workbench, trying to rebuild the carburetor of an old pick-up truck, using small wrenches and screwdrivers to replace the jets — painstaking, greasy work. Dad enters with a sack lunch and thermos, stops a short distance from Rafe.)*

DAD. What are you doing there?

RAFE. Gonna get that truck going.

DAD. Well, I hope Jesus Christ and Moses and all the twelve apostles is gonna come down and piss on that truck, 'cause that's what it'll take to get her going again.

RAFE. *(Eyes on his work.)* I'll get her going. *(Dad makes his disgusted gesture, but keeps watching another moment. Then:)*

DAD. Well, you don't give up easy, I'll say that for ya. *(No response. Brief pause.)*

RAFE. I'm moving out.

DAD. Good. What kept ya?

RAFE. *(Beat.)* You can still cut me deep, you old son of a bitch.

DAD. *(Regrets his words but can't say so.)* Who you calling old? *(Beat; no response.)* I ain't saying I know how to talk to you or ever did.

RAFE. That's for damn sure.

DAD. Aw, shut up. *(Brief pause.)* I gotta go to work. And you better get your tail out and find yourself a job.

RAFE. I told you what I'm gonna do, I'm gonna get that land back —

DAD. Now just don't talk so goddamn stupid, Rafe. Do what you *can* do in this world, and don't go getting tangled up in fairy stories. *(No response. Approaching the bench, Dad sets down the sack, opens the thermos.)* You want a little pick-me-up?

RAFE. No, thanks.

DAD. There's coffee in it too, for all you know. *(Pours coffee-whiskey mix into the thermos cup, drinks, then:)* I'm gonna give you some of Granddad's land.

RAFE. *(Stunned. Beat; then.)* I thought you sold it all.

DAD. The farmland and the pasture land, I did. But there's all that timberland leading up to hunting camp. Close to fifty acres. I'll give you ten.

RAFE. I couldn't farm that land.

DAD. *(Laughs.)* Hell, no. Your granddad used to say, "It's so steep back there, you'd have to harness the thunder and lightning to haul 'em up top."

RAFE. What good is it?

DAD. ... It's family land. Build a cabin, where our old hunting cabin used to be ... before they burned it down, whoever them bastards was....

RAFE. I'm gonna farm.

DAD. ... He's gonna farm. Well, goodness to mercy, you go right on and do that. You break your back cutting down and hauling trees, and hauling boulders, and clearing out the poison ivy and the nettles and the skunks and snakes ... it's your land, you have yourself a time, suffering all over it. *(Starts to exit.)*

RAFE. I ain't gonna farm it. But I'll take it. *(Dad stops, looks at him, maybe hoping for some connection. Rafe regards him stonily.)*

DAD. "Never give nothing." That's you, ain't it?

RAFE. It is now. *(Crossfade as Dad and Rafe exit; the bench is cleared. Dylan enters with a spade. He's been digging holes for trees, flops on the ground, sweaty and exhausted. Rafe reenters, wary but drawn.)* 'Lo.

DYLAN. ... Hey, how you doing?

RAFE. I see you're planting trees here.

DYLAN. Right. Man, it's a bitch.

RAFE. My family's been clearing this land for a hundred years. Now you're planting trees on it.

DYLAN. Oh, you're Ruby's brother? I'm Dylan. *(Offers his hand. They shake.)* They aren't my idea. The trees. I just work for him.

RAFE. What's he want more trees for?

DYLAN. Sell 'em later. Christmas trees. I think it's a tax thing ... I dunno. Like I said —

RAFE. We're sitting in the middle of a forest.

DYLAN. Guess the tax guys don't know that. Or don't care.

RAFE. What else is he gonna do?

DYLAN. Well ... he wants to make a pond or something over in the meadow. *(Indicates the meadow area in the audience.)*

RAFE. A pond? What for?

DYLAN. *(Shrugs.)* Swim in it?

RAFE. We got swimming holes all around here.

DYLAN. Maybe that's a tax thing too. Or else it'll increase the resale value —

RAFE. Resale?

DYLAN. I'm just guessing. He doesn't tell me stuff like that. But there's a bunch of turtles that hang out in the pond. I don't know what'll happen to them if it goes.

RAFE. Them mud turtles. I seen 'em since I was a kid. *(Brief pause. Abruptly.)* That meadow oughta have horses in it.

DYLAN. That's what I think too. But this guy I work for, Brooks ... seems like an okay guy, you know ... but he hardly ever comes up here. And when he does, he gets the backhoe itch.

RAFE. Them city guys. They'd move Slide Mountain, put it on the other side of Hightop.

DYLAN. *(Laughs.)* That's it. Me, I like it around here. Like it the way it *is.*

RAFE. *(Warming to Dylan.)* If I had my way, none of the crap that come in since I was a kid'd be here. I'd like to see trees growing up through the Walmart parking lot.

DYLAN. *(Laughs.)* Right ... yeah, that'd be great, wouldn't it?

RAFE. I gotta talk to him before he starts bringing them backhoes in ... you know Ruby?

DYLAN. ... Yeah, uh-huh....

RAFE. *(Looks at him a beat; abruptly.)* See that ridge up there above the stand of pine trees?

DYLAN. ... Yeah....

RAFE. That's where I'm living now. You can find me there and let me know when he comes up again.

DYLAN. Okay.

RAFE. I'm gonna buy that meadow back, keep my horses in it.

DYLAN. Great! What kind of horses have you got?

RAFE. Ain't got 'em yet.

DYLAN. Oh.

RAFE. Not yet. But I will. *(Rafe exits, leaving Dylan puzzled and amused. Crossfade to Rafe's camp, night. Rafe and Julie enter, Rafe using a flashlight to lead the way along a path. He wears a backpack. Julie wears a cute outfit and high-heeled sandals, carries a tote bag. She's being bitten by mosquitoes and stumbling over rocks and roots.)*

JULIE. *(Trips.)* Shit!

RAFE. Well, why'dya want to wear them shoes?

JULIE. How'd *I* know it'd be this rough? There's hardly a trail, even.

RAFE. That's why my dad give me this land. He can't sell it 'cause it's on the back side of a mountain. Nobody in his right mind'd trouble to build on it.

JULIE. *(Rueful.)* But that ain't stopping you.

RAFE. I ain't building here. I'm just squatting, temporary. You know where I'm gonna build.

JULIE. In the meadow.

RAFE. Sure. Well, on the rise ... looking down on the meadow. I wanta be able to see that big old rock and them two little branches of the creek from my bedroom window. *(Pause.)* You want something to drink?

JULIE. Okay. *(Slaps a mosquito.)*

RAFE. Got Coke and 7-Up in the stream there, keeps it nice and cold. Got a watermelon too.

JULIE. You hauled a watermelon up here? *(Looks at him; no response, so:)* How 'bout a beer?

RAFE. Don't keep it around.

JULIE. One beer ain't gonna hurt you, Rafe.

RAFE. You know my dad, you know why I'd rather not get into it.

JULIE. I'll take a Coke. *(Slaps a mosquito.)*

RAFE. Put some of that bug stuff on, it's in my pack.

JULIE. I don't want to smell like that tonight....

RAFE. Okay, get bit. *(Rafe exits. Crossfade. In moonlight, Ruby and Dylan sit on the floor of an otherwise empty attic in the old farmhouse.)*

RUBY. Tell me some more about your travels. Like about that old hotel in Mexico with all the birds.

DYLAN. I'm gonna run out of stories pretty soon.

RUBY. You better not.

DYLAN. Oh, that's all you're coming around for, huh?

RUBY. *(Looks at him, letting him wonder, then:)* What's your favorite place you've ever been?

DYLAN. *(Beat; saying what she wants to hear.)* The next place.

RUBY. *(Delighted.)* Yeah? Where'll that be?

DYLAN. Won't know till I get there.

RUBY. That's it! That's what *I* want!

DYLAN. Why not? *(He holds her gaze: a powerful connection. Brief pause. Ruby breaks it, turns away.)*

RUBY. Funny, being up here in the attic. I used to play in here when I was little. And my dad talks about it sometimes ... how it was when he was growing up in this house, and even what it musta been like way back in the old days, when my great-great-grandparents homesteaded here. They had twenty-two kids in this house. Don't know where they put 'em all ... well, a lot of 'em died, though.

DYLAN. Maybe they're still around.

RUBY. Where, here?

DYLAN. Perfect place for 'em. Their old home sold off to a stranger. They're gonna hang around till the one true rightful family is living in the house again.

RUBY. They're gonna get tired of waiting.

DYLAN. Ssshhhhh ... you'll get 'em all riled up. *(Leans close, makes ghost-like noises.)*

RUBY. *(Laughs.)* Quit that, you!

DYLAN. Doesn't it bother you?

RUBY. *(Scornfully.)* What, ghosts?

DYLAN. Losing your family's house and land. It sure bothers your brother.

RUBY. ... A little bit, I guess. But my dad's right, land that don't make money is just a stone around your neck. Let somebody else pay the taxes. Anyway, who wants to farm? You can't never get away! My dad says when this whole country was nothing but farmers, and a killing frost was coming, the church bells would ring in the middle of the night, and people would get out of bed and gather all the blankets and clothes in the whole house to cover up the crops, so they wouldn't all die that same night.

DYLAN. ... Wow ... that's *real,* you know?

RUBY. But, Dylan! Farmers gotta be around *all the time* for stuff like that! I ain't gonna get stuck like that, nowhere, no how, no way. I'm gonna go everywhere, see everything, like you.

DYLAN. Well, don't leave just yet, okay?

RUBY. Same to you. *(She holds his gaze, challenging him. Abruptly, she kisses him passionately. Crossfade to Rafe and Julie. Rafe returns with a bottle of Coke and firewood, gives the Coke to Julie.)*

RAFE. Gonna make a fire. Keep the bugs off.

JULIE. That'd be nice. *(Slaps a mosquito on her thigh.)*

RAFE. Here, put this on your legs. *(He hands her his jacket. She wraps it around her legs. Rafe builds a fire. Julie watches. Brief pause, then:)*

JULIE. I got promoted.
RAFE. Good for you.
JULIE. My boss says I've got a real good future there. Says he's lucky to have me.
RAFE. Smart guy.
JULIE. So I asked him would he pay for me to take some courses at the CC —
RAFE. At the what?
JULIE. The community college.
RAFE. Oh. Right....
JULIE. And he said he would. So in the fall I'm gonna go to school three nights a week. I'm gonna take advanced computer science and French.
RAFE. You're on your way, sounds like.
JULIE. That's right, I am. I don't want to live in a trailer all my life.
RAFE. Your folks done the best they could.
JULIE. People ain't meant to live in trailers, Rafe. Not in America.
RAFE. Well, you're doing what you gotta do for yourself, just like I am. I respect you, you know that.
JULIE. *(Beat.)* I brought you some stuff, here. *(Opens her tote bag.)*
RAFE. *(Teasing.)* Uh-oh. It ain't candy and cookies and razor blades, is it?
JULIE. Shut up. It's food, though. I just thought ... you roughing it up here ... maybe I'd bring you something special.... *(Julie spreads a cloth, lays out pretty paper plates, matching napkins, grapes, a little cheese knife, a box of French crackers and two slabs of cheese. Meanwhile:)*
RAFE. This ain't so rough. Had it a whole lot rougher when I hunted with my dad. Up here, I got a latrine, even. Dug it myself. Only thing they taught me in the army that come in handy. Had to dig it twice, though. Spent all day digging an eight-foot hole and then I didn't cover it and it rained all night. Filled up the whole damn hole in one damn night. Had to dig another one just to get even. *(As Julie laughs.)* Now don't you never tell that story on me. If my dad come to hear about

it, he'd tell it on me every day till the day he died. *(Rafe kneels to light the fire: lighting effect. He looks at the food, picks up the cracker box.)* What're they getting at here?

JULIE. It's in French. They're French crackers.

RAFE. ... Uh-huh.... *(Picks up a slab of brie.)*

JULIE. That's French cheese too. Brie, that one is. It's real good.

RAFE. Looks pretty well cooked down here, Julie.

JULIE. That's how it's supposed to be. "Runny," that's the way they like it.

RAFE. ... Well, at least it ain't pre-sliced in them little envelopes.

JULIE. This is the classy stuff! I would've brought some wine, they always have wine with their meals in France, but I figured you wouldn't drink it.

RAFE. You figured right. Where'd you get wine anyway? You ain't twenty-one.

JULIE. ... I can get it when I want to.

RAFE. From your boss, or who? *(No response. Picking up the other cheese.)* This one must be a reject — it ain't runny.

JULIE. It ain't the runny type — it's chevre.

RAFE. "Shevrah?" ... *(Opens the wrapper to sniff the cheese.)* What's that mean?

JULIE. *(Reluctantly.)* ... Goat cheese — but it's good, go on and try it —

RAFE. *(Laughs.)* Goat cheese! Hell, my grandma used to make that stuff and us kids wouldn't eat it. We played with them goats, we knew 'em. They'd eat anything from poison ivy to chicken shit —

JULIE. Well, fine! You can spend the rest of your life living in a tent and eating Ritz Crackers!

RAFE. Nothing wrong with Ritz Crackers. Charlton Heston eats 'em. You're the one who told me that —

JULIE. Well, I can't live my life on 'em! I gotta go to work in an office every day, and I gotta look my best! I gotta wear nice stockings that don't have ladders in 'em, not to mention twigs and burrs, and I gotta shower and shampoo my hair every day and mousse it and blow-dry it and put my makeup on —

RAFE. All for this boss of yours? Lotta trouble, seems to me —

JULIE. It's for him and me and everyone who's living out there in the world — it's how we live now, Rafe! And I can't do all the stuff I gotta do to get ahead, if I hafta live in a tent and piss in a latrine and hike a two-mile trail just to get to my car, can I?

RAFE. Who asked you to? *(Julie starts to cry. Shocked, Rafe doesn't know what to do. Awkwardly, touching her.)* ... Julie, I'm just teasing you....

JULIE. ... I thought ... I thought you....

RAFE. ... What?

JULIE. You know!... I thought you wanted me around.

RAFE. ... I do....

JULIE. ... All the time, I mean....

RAFE. ... Well ... I got things to do, I got a hard row to hoe, and —

JULIE. You're *making* it a hard row! You don't have to do all this — you could do *anything!* Rafe, all's we gotta do is get on the same road together. We can have a real good life — 'cause the opportunities are out there, I just know it! *(Rafe can't answer — he doesn't want the life she wants. He keeps stroking her back. She quiets, knowing argument is futile, but she's deeply unhappy. Still stroking her back:)*

RAFE. D'I tell you I bought a team of draft horses?

JULIE. ... You told me. *(Beat.)* I shouldn'ta waited for you.

RAFE. Don't say that. I'm glad you waited. *(Gently, he embraces her, kisses her. She responds. Crossfade to the porch of the old farmhouse: a couple of wicker chairs, a small table, a screen door leading off into the house. Evan Brooks enters the porch, arriving from the city, with an expensive briefcase and a paper deli bag. Dylan hurries out to meet him, flustered, striving for his usual easy charm.)*

DYLAN. Hi, Mr. Brooks, good to see you —

BROOKS. Hey, Dylan, I see you got those trees in.

DYLAN. Yeah, they look real nice too. Can I help you, have you got some other stuff — ?

BROOKS. Nah, this is it, I'm just here overnight. Got a van coming up with some furniture tomorrow. Can you be around for that?

DYLAN. Oh sure, no problem. *(Brooks sets the deli bag on the small table and the briefcase on the floor.)*

BROOKS. Great. You know, we never talked about your hours when I'm up here.

DYLAN. Oh, well ... fine, whatever....

BROOKS. *(Taking a wrapped sandwich out of the bag.)* Well, usually I'd say you can take off most of the time I'm here, go visit friends, stay all night, have fun ... I'd like the privacy too, frankly ...

DYLAN. *(Uneasy: where would he go?)* Oh ... oh, sure....

BROOKS. ... but this van is coming pretty early in the morning. *(Sees his sandwich is shedding.)* Oops, I'm making kind of a mess, here....

DYLAN. You want a plate or something? And napkins? I could —

BROOKS. No, I'll get it — I think I left some beer here too — *(Brooks starts for the screen door. Dylan gets in his path, eager to intercept him.)*

DYLAN. Yeah, you did — no, really, let me get it — I gotta admit, I got a few dishes piled up in there — *(Ruby comes out of the house, looking tousled, like she just got out of bed. She's embarrassed, but has decided to carry it off.)*

RUBY. Hi, Mr. Brooks. I'm here too.

BROOKS. *(Amused, impressed with Ruby.)* Oh ... oh, okay ... hello ... *(Juggles sandwich, shakes hands with her.)* Evan Brooks.

RUBY. Ruby Carroll. My dad sold you this house.

BROOKS. I've seen you, but we haven't met. Well, nice to meet you, Ruby.

DYLAN. Ruby wanted to look around the old place —

BROOKS. Sure, sure. Any time.

RUBY. I ain't been inside here in a lot of years. When my granddad got sick, he moved in with us and my dad closed this place up. Glad somebody bought it ... maybe even have kids playing in it again.

BROOKS. Not mine. I mean, I'm not married.... Well, I'm going to get a beer ... Ruby, would you like — ?

RUBY. Oh, sure.

BROOKS. Dylan...?

DYLAN. Uh, sure, thanks a lot.... *(Brooks goes into the farmhouse. Dylan and Ruby give each other "Oh my God!" looks, laughing silently. Whispering.)* I don't believe this! You've got him waiting on you!

RUBY. *(Playfully airy.)* Why don't you believe it? *(Dylan laughs, proud of her, reaches for her. She smiles, evades him teasingly, sits demurely. Playing "casual.")* I coulda combed my hair, I guess.... *(Dylan loves this. Brooks comes back out with three expensive imported beers. Dylan quickly takes two of them and hands one to Ruby.)*

DYLAN. Thanks a lot. Want me to get that plate for you — ?

BROOKS. No, I'll eat later — I need to relax.

RUBY. Well, you come to the right place. It's so relaxing around here, you're like to fall asleep.

BROOKS. *(Amused.)* Tired of country life?

RUBY. What life? There's the mall and the dirt track. And skinny-dipping in the summer — that's the *real* big thrill.

BROOKS. ... But it's beautiful country.

RUBY. Yeah, well, trees is trees.

BROOKS. Sounds like you're a city girl. Get down there much?

RUBY. Couple times on high school trips is all. My dad thinks it's the hell-and-damnationville.

BROOKS. He's not far wrong.

RUBY. I bet things are changing every minute down there.

BROOKS. Sometimes it kind of wears you out.

RUBY. Ain't nothing ever changes here, unless somebody's house burns down. I'll get to the city one of these days, and I ain't coming back.

BROOKS. You should check it out first.

RUBY. ... Yeah, I guess....

BROOKS. If you decide to come down for a visit, call me. I could show you around a little.

RUBY. *(Hiding her amazement.)* Oh ... well ... thanks....

BROOKS. Here, I'll give you my card. *(Stunned silence as he takes out his wallet, opens it. Ruby and Dylan try not to stare at the money and credit cards as Brooks extracts a card, hands it to Ruby.)* Give me a few weeks notice, things are always hectic. But sure

... the city seems pretty grim to me these days. It might be nice to see it through your eyes.... *(Dylan wills Ruby to look at him. She stares into space and drinks beer. A moment of silence, then:)* Well. I've got more phone calls to make tonight. *(Hands Dylan his empty bottle, takes the deli food and starts to exit.)* See you in the morning, Dylan — bright and early, right?

DYLAN. Right.

BROOKS. *(To Ruby.)* Will I see you, too?

DYLAN. Oh, no, no, she's not living here or anything.... *(Ruby gives Dylan a cool look. Both men pick up on it.)*

RUBY. *(To Brooks.)* No, I'm not living here or *anything.*

BROOKS. Ah. Well, see you, then. *(Brooks exits. Ruby swigs the dregs of beer, not meeting Dylan's look. He listens, makes sure Brooks is really gone, then.)*

DYLAN. *(Softly.)* What was that?

RUBY. What was what?

DYLAN. "I'm not living here or a*nything.*"

RUBY. Well, how 'bout you? Apologizing for me —

DYLAN. I was not apologizing, I was —

RUBY. Kissing his ass —

DYLAN. Like hell! I just, I need this job —

RUBY. Thought you was passing through. *(Brief pause.)*

DYLAN. You're not gonna take him up on it, are you?

RUBY. Why not?

DYLAN. ... What would you want to do that for?

RUBY. Why not? *(Dylan looks at her a beat, starts to turn away toward the farmhouse, holding the two bottles.)* Dylan? *(He turns back. She hands him her empty bottle as if he's a servant. He takes it automatically, then has an uprush of anger — she laughs: Gotcha! Furious, he wheels to go out. She's on her feet, wraps her arms around him from behind, presses herself against him. Dylan freezes, then mimes a fierce over-the-shoulder movement of braining her with a beer bottle. Laughing joyously.)* I don't know as I'd blame you.

DYLAN. ... Nobody'd blame me.

RUBY. *(Softly, nuzzling him.)* I just don't want you to go thinking this is easy.

DYLAN. No danger of that.

RUBY. Don't be mad. I chose you. *(Beat; Dylan slowly turns in her arms as she clings to him. Face to face.)*

DYLAN. Ruby, what do you want from me?

RUBY. *(Passionately, full of hope.)* Take me with you! Get me out! *(He drops the bottles, kisses her wildly. She pulls him down to the floor, responding passionately.)*

DYLAN. *(Making crazy love but still protesting.)* We can't — not here — he's right upstairs —

RUBY. *(Pulling his shirt off.)* ... I love you, Dylan.... *(Dylan loses control, is making love to her with all his frustration and need. Crossfade to the Carrolls' yard. Mom and Julie stand at a small table with a big bowl of whole peaches on it. They're cutting up the peaches for a pie.)*

JULIE. *(Hoping for reassurance.)* It ain't like Rafe has another girl. It ain't ... it isn't like he doesn't care about me ... I don't think....

MOM. Oh, no....

JULIE. But he doesn't listen. He doesn't even think about what I say.

MOM. I know it. That's just how they are. When I was a girl, and Marlin come looking out for me, he wouldn't do *nothing* I wanted. Wouldn't change his shoes for me. He'd come see me in his work boots, all gunked up with manure and mud ... and he *wanted* me.

JULIE. *Yeah* ... so ... how...?

MOM. He was a handsome boy.

JULIE. He still is. Damn him anyway.

MOM. Marlin.

JULIE. ... Oh....

MOM. You don't see it now. But he was. And men around here, mostly they don't talk. But Marlin, he told stories good as I ever heard. And quick — he had a way of turning what you said around on you ... but it wasn't mean then, it was ... we had good times in them days. He built our house at night while he was working full days on the propane truck. He'd come home dog-tired and eat some supper and then start to work again, pouring cement or laying joists. Come dark, I'd hold the flashlight for him so he could see to work. Sometimes we'd be real close like that and he'd say, "Ceelie, put that flashlight down ..." *(Julie is embarrassed — a parent talking about sex! Mom is away for a moment. Then:)* But stubborn. Stubborn. Wouldn't go out of his way ... wouldn't take nothing back ... not for me or nobody ... till Ruby come along.

JULIE. Ruby ... yeah.

MOM. Right from the first, she owned him. Making him go here and there, like she was driving team.*

JULIE. Wish I could do that even once —

MOM. You can't. You gotta be like Ruby and her dad. And we ain't like them. *(Crossfade to the yard of the old farmhouse. Dylan enters, carrying a heavy piece of furniture. He stops just onstage, sets it down and rests. Julie exits. Mom enters the farmhouse area, watching Dylan from a little distance. She struggles against a violent impulse, loses, blurts.)* Hey, you.

DYLAN. *(Surprised.)* Oh, hi.

MOM. ... What you doing?

DYLAN. Just hauling some furniture. *(Mom moves closer to Dylan, slowly, as if drawn.)*

MOM. Looks like thirsty work.

DYLAN. Yeah ... kinda hot already.

MOM. *(Can't help herself.)* Come on up to the house and have a cold drink.

DYLAN. *(Beat.)* The house?

MOM. Right up the road, there.

DYLAN. ... You're Ruby's mom? Nice to meet you, Mrs. Carroll. *(He extends a hand. Mom slowly takes it.)*

MOM. I'm Ceelie.

DYLAN. I'm Dylan.

MOM. I know. Pretty name. *(Mom stares down at their clasped hands, shyly, but can't let go. Dylan starts to feel that something else is going on here, and he's thrown. Gently, he extricates his hand as:)*

DYLAN. *(Delicately.)* Is Ruby...? Is she home or...?

MOM. *(Shy but tenacious.)* No. She's at work. So's her dad. It's real quiet up there. And cool, I keep the house dark when it's hot like this, so it stays nice and cool inside. I got cold

* "Driving team" is an old country expression for driving a team of horses or oxen.

things to drink. *(As always, Dylan is pulled toward giving someone what she wants. But he can't screw things up with Ruby and Brooks. As he hesitates, Brooks enters from the farmhouse with a mug of coffee. Mom instantly moves away from Dylan, who's relieved.)*

DYLAN. *(To Mom.)* Well, thanks, but my boss needs me to help him out. *(Mom exits, in turmoil, relieved and disappointed.)* But really, thanks ... sometime I'd really like that.... *(Starts to pick up the piece of furniture.)*

BROOKS. Hold on a sec, I'll finish my coffee and give you a hand ... who was that?

DYLAN. Ruby's mom.

BROOKS. Ah ... sure didn't take you long to find the prettiest girl around. Ruby seems so sure of herself too ... for someone that young....

DYLAN. ... Yeah....

BROOKS. How old is she, do you know?

DYLAN. ... She just got out of high school. Eighteen, seventeen, in there....

BROOKS. Eighteen? She'll be dangerous in a few years.

DYLAN. Dangerous?

BROOKS. But she's too young yet, and ... well ... rough around the edges.

DYLAN. *(Relieved.)* Oh, well, sure....

BROOKS. *(Abruptly.)* So if she does call me, I think I'll meet her in the city. Can't hurt, right?

DYLAN. *(Very thrown.)* ... Sure ... right....

BROOKS. I should probably talk to her parents about it. Let them know it's all highly respectable ... I bet they watch her like a hawk.

DYLAN. I bet.

BROOKS. Do they?

DYLAN. Well ... I don't know, really.

BROOKS. They'd be crazy not to. *(Dylan is afraid to assert his rights to Ruby, but he makes an effort.)*

DYLAN. She's ... we're seeing each other, you know ... but ... she'd make up her own mind anyway....

BROOKS. She made that clear. Let's lug that thing inside. *(Brooks sets down his mug to help move the furniture as Rafe enters, intercepting Dylan.)*

RAFE. *(Softly.)* You said you was gonna come and tell me when he showed up here.

DYLAN. *(Softly.)* He got in late last night. You didn't expect me to climb up there in the dark, did you?

RAFE. I do it all the time.

DYLAN. Well, look, don't ... just take it easy, okay? *(Brooks joins Dylan. Rafe extends his hand to Brooks, they shake.)*

RAFE. Rafe Carroll.

BROOKS. Evan Brooks. You're Ruby's brother?

RAFE. *(Looks at Dylan, back at Brooks.)* That's right, Mr. Brooks, and I'll get right to the point. Nothing against you, but I can't go along with my dad selling out the family land.

BROOKS. *(Beat.)* Your name's not on the title...?

RAFE. I don't have no legal rights. It goes beyond that.

BROOKS. ... Oh. Well, I can see that you might feel —

RAFE. It ain't how I feel. It's what I'm gonna do. I'm gonna buy my own land back from you.

BROOKS. *(Beat.)* Do you know what I paid your father for this property?

RAFE. No, but it's gotta be more than I can raise just all at once. So I wanta start by buying this here meadow. I got a team of draft horses, big beautiful animals, I wanta turn 'em out to graze right here where they belong. So how much would you take for it?

BROOKS. For the meadow?

RAFE. Yeah. Clear up to the tree line.

BROOKS. I really couldn't sell it for less than a hundred thousand.

RAFE. *(Speechless. Finally:)* It ain't even twelve acres.

BROOKS. Right. But I haven't decided whether I'm going to live on this property or develop it —

RAFE. Develop it?

BROOKS. There's great potential. If I had a big pond dug, built three, four at the most, houses around the pond ... upscale housing, cedar decks, local bluestone chimneys....

RAFE. You can't sell houses now. Every highway and back road is nothing but "For Sale" signs!

BROOKS. In the long run, land values only rise. You just have to wait the rough times out. Your dad sold at a bad time. But I couldn't make the same mistake.
RAFE. So you're gonna stick to that. A hundred thousand.
BROOKS. That would be rock-bottom. And I'd have to be sure that however *you* develop it, it would increase the value of the rest of my property —
RAFE. I ain't gonna develop beans. I'm gonna leave it whole.
BROOKS. Well, you'll use it for something, won't you? *(Rafe can't believe he has to explain to this stranger. He looks at Dylan, meets a blank wall. Long beat; then.)*
RAFE. Graze my horses.
BROOKS. So you'd have to fence it.
RAFE. ... Sure ... tall, stout fence ... water trough ... little stable, for the weather. Outside the fence, prob'ly put a garden in. Out toward the rise there ... maybe in a couple years, put a house up there....
BROOKS. Well, all that might be charming, or it might be an eyesore, depends on how you do it. As I said, I'm sympathetic, but this is what I do, and I can't do it badly just to make you feel better. I'm sure *you* understand *that.*
RAFE. *(Beat.)* To a point, I do.
BROOKS. Sorry, Rafe. Look, I'll make you a deal. You raise the money and draw up a specific proposal of how you'd use the land, and we'll talk about it. Okay? *(Claps Rafe on the back. To Dylan.)* Let's go. Heave-ho. *(Brooks and Dylan exit with the furniture. Crossfade to Ruby and Darlene, walking toward McDonald's across a parking lot. They carry their bags, wear their caps at rakish angles. Darlene is fervently smoking in the last moments before she'll have to stub it out. Ruby is thinking of Dylan and half-listening to Darlene.)*
RUBY. ... You shoulda called the cops on him.
DARLENE. Oh, sure! Then how'd I raise the money to bail him out? Go around all begging to everybody who don't have no money anyway ... or not for Dale, they don't ... I know I oughta dump him, I know you're gonna say that, but....
RUBY. ... You gotta do what you gotta do. *(Puzzled, Darlene looks at her. Hoping to hook her interest.)*

DARLENE. You shoulda seen Lisa last night at the Lounge. She's got some French-fried nerve. Had her big old butt squeezed into them tight, shiny bicycle pants. And her hair looked like a rat sucked it.

RUBY. ... Lisa ain't so bad.

DARLENE. Since when? Since you got tired of Lance? *(Lance appears, following Ruby and drinking a beer in a paper bag.)*

RUBY. *(Indifferent.)* They'll prob'ly be real good together. "Lance and Lisa," I can see it on the matchbooks.

DARLENE. Ruby, what the hell? Where *are* you? *(Ruby's smile gives her away. Lance slowly comes nearer. He wants her to see him.)*

RUBY. I just feel good is all.

DARLENE. My ass! It's that whoever-whatsit you been seeing without admitting nothing lately — what's his name? When do I get to meet him? *(Ruby is laughing, shushing her. She looks around, sees Lance, squeezes Darlene's arm.)* Ow! Shit! What — ? *(Sees Lance.)*

RUBY	DARLENE
Hi, Lance.	Hey, Lance, how's it hangin'?

LANCE. So what's his name?

RUBY. ... Say what?

LANCE. Don't bother. I seen you in the woods with him. *(Ruby is embarrassed, but clings to her cool.)*

DARLENE. Lance, we gotta get into work —

LANCE. So git. *(Darlene hesitates. Ruby shrugs. Darlene stubs out her cigarette. To Ruby but warning Lance.)*

DARLENE. The manager's prob'ly watching through the window there, you better hurry up. *(She exits. Beat.)*

RUBY. So you've seen me with him. So?

LANCE. You can't treat me like shit —

RUBY. I don't owe you nothing.

LANCE. Bullshit!... You was damn glad to be with me till he came along. And I ain't no different. I'm still kicking ass at the dirt track every Saturday and taking home that prize money —

RUBY. It ain't just him. I grew up, that's all. *(Lance has a violent impulse to sock her. She sees it and flinches. They both glance toward the McDonald's windows.)* The manager sees you drinking, he'll come out and run you off —

LANCE. Just let him try, I'll kick his fucking head in. *(Brief pause. Almost an appeal.)* I got a sponsor, Ruby.

RUBY. Who?

LANCE. Quincy's Tavern. They're gonna back me to move up to the half-mile track. And if I make it there, I can go out on the circuit! No more dragging some old wreck outa the woods and building her from the ground up, just so's I could race ... knowing I never had no chance at the half-mile track, 'cause the high-dollar cars'd win it even if them guys couldn't drive a nail.... A custom-built car, Ruby! Gonna go to driving school and learn all them techniques I can't learn on my own, 'cause nobody I ever seen up close knows shit ... now I can show what I can do!

RUBY. *(Impressed.)* Well, that's great.

LANCE. And you're the one kept telling me I had to move up or die. Well, now I'm moving up. And you can come along. You can travel with me. Go down to Florida in the winter for the nationals —

RUBY. You sure about this, Lance? You seen their money yet?

LANCE. ... We shook on it. They can't go back on me.

RUBY. Well ... I mean, Quincy's Tavern, they ain't much. How they gonna come up with enough money for all that stuff? You're hanging your hat on a small peg if you think —

LANCE. Shut up, now!... That's your old man talking in your mouth, that ain't you talking, Ruby. *(Touching her gently.)* ... If you stood by me ... Ruby ... I think about you —

RUBY. *(Shrugging him off.)* Don't. Just don't think about me. Any day now, I'll be outa here. And Lisa, she'll be good for you.

LANCE. You ain't going nowhere.

RUBY. *(Beat; coolly.)* I ain't afraid of you. *(She turns to go. He grabs her arm, hurting her. She gasps, is motionless as Lance, behind her, moves in close.)*

LANCE. What if I had my gun? *(Darlene races out, in uniform, screaming.)*

DARLENE. LANCE, YOU GET ON OUTA HERE, THE

MANAGER'S CALLING THE COPS! *(Tries to pry Lance's hand off Ruby's arm.)* Come on, I ain't kidding, the cops're coming — *(Lance shoves Darlene away, scaring her. Still holding Ruby, he kisses the back of her neck, lets go of her and exits.)* Jesus! Did he hurt you?

RUBY. *(Shaken, shakes her head no.)* ... Was everybody watching?

DARLENE. Are you kidding? Them golden-agers like to fall outa their chairs! You're gonna have a bruise — I know. Listen, you need a drink, and I got that peach schnapps hid in by the frying vats —

RUBY. *(Shakes her head no.)* ... Let's get on in. *(They head offstage. Crossfade to Rafe's camp, night. Rafe and Dylan are sitting by the fire.)*

RAFE. First time my dad took me hunting, I was twelve years old. We come up here to camp, the two of us, and we took our guns and went deep into the woods. Dad sat on a big rock, so I sat beside him. And we sat there, holding our guns, and ready. Seemed like hours. Dad didn't move a muscle, so I didn't either. Got real hungry, had to piss bad — but I didn't move. *(Beat.)*

Then I seen her, a big pretty doe, maybe thirty yards away. She was coming through the brush and walking straight at us, with that almost floating look they got on them twiggy legs, but you can see the strength in 'em too ... Dad, he didn't move. And then I seen another doe behind her, and another, and another, coming toward us in a line, like we'd called 'em to us. But Dad still didn't move. *(Beat.)*

I was getting wild inside, sweating through my clothes — wild to get a clear shot while I had at least a chance of getting my first deer, showing Dad what I could do. But he was so still, I couldn't even feel his breathing, up close against him like I was, and I couldn't do nothing but what he would do ... till there was thirteen doe coming toward us, and the closest one I swore was gonna come right up to me and nuzzle me for sugar ... and Dad still didn't move. *(Beat.)*

And then he moved so quick, I hadn't hardly felt him move 'fore I heard his gun crack out and seen that big buck fall — that big six-pointer coming at the end of the line of doe, like Dad knowed he would do. He got him. I seen him fall. Them doe were scattering everywhere, and we just watched 'em go. I said, "You got him, Dad!" And my dad said, "Well, I did, didn't I?" *(Long beat; then:)* After that ... I was wild to go hunting ... hunting with my dad. *(Brief pause.)*

DYLAN. Yeah, that's ... I never looked at it that way ... that's cool....

RAFE. *(Beat.)* 'Preciate you coming up to see me. Mostly folks don't bother.

DYLAN. Oh, no, hey, I can really see this. I love being in the woods.

RAFE. Me too. I like the sounds. That's why I ain't got a radio. Or a clock neither. Tell time by the sun. Close enough. *(Brief pause.)* Want some more of that brie cheese?

DYLAN. No, thanks. It's good, though.

RAFE. It ain't too bad with Ritz Crackers. *(Pause.)*

DYLAN. Ruby said you've got a girlfriend.

RAFE. Well, she don't come up here if she's got her stockings on.... She's going out, some. Playing the field. *(Brief pause.)*

DYLAN. So what do you guys do at night around here? Besides this, I mean. Ruby says there's nothing, but there's gotta be *something,* right?

RAFE. If you drink ... you drink.

DYLAN. ... Uh-huh....

RAFE. Go to the V.I.P. Lounge ... play pool ... or there's the dirt track....

DYLAN. Yeah, I'd like to check that out.

RAFE. It's loud. *(Pause. Dylan waits. That's it.)*

DYLAN. I was kind of wondering ... the nights are getting cold already. Are you going to try to stay up here in winter ... or...?

RAFE. *(Long beat; then:)* My dad told me about one time my granddad drove a team up here when the snow was so deep, it took him half a day to make it to the cabin. And it was deep cold too. But Granddad come ahead, 'cause he was gonna meet his crew and help 'em do some logging. And my dad come along. He was just a kid. He said it was so durn cold, he was afraid he'd freeze to death sitting in the wagon, but he knew my granddad and he never said a word. When they made it up here, wasn't nobody around logging. Come to find out, the crew was all huddled up inside the cabin, burning all the wood. Said it was too durn cold to work. Granddad was so disgusted, he took and threw a load of wood up on the wagon, told my dad to climb aboard, and they went right straight back. *(Pause. Blam! Sound offstage of a high-powered rifle shot. Rafe hits the ground.)* Get down! *(Dylan hits the ground. Another shot. Yells toward the sounds.)* HEY, THERE'S FOLKS UP HERE, QUIT SHOOTING! *(Silence. Pause. Rafe starts to rise. Another shot, closer. He hits the ground again.)* HEY, GET THE FUCK OUTA HERE!!! *(They listen. Sound of branches breaking underfoot.)*

DYLAN. He's not going away.

RAFE. Some asshole trying to prove something.... *(Rafe pulls himself along the ground to his gear, unearths his rifle. Another shot, closer yet.)*

DYLAN. Jesus, who *is* that guy? Think maybe some psycho escaped from the prison?... Or has someone got a grudge against you?...

RAFE. Just my dad. *(Dylan laughs nervously, then screams as Lance roars into camp, wildly drunk, whooping and waving his high-powered hunting rifle. He falls over Rafe and Dylan, gets entangled with them. His rifle smacks the ground hard and goes off — a deafening blam! Stunned silence, then:)*

LANCE. *(Laughing.)* ... Whoa, shit....

RAFE. *(Grabs the gun.) "Shit?!"* ... You ... you ... shit-for-brains!! What the fuck are you doing here?!

LANCE. I just miscounted, I thought it was empty — chill out, you ain't hurt none.... *(Rafe checks — now the gun is empty. He throws it on the ground, grabs Lance, enraged.)*

RAFE. Don't you never ... don't you never in your life ... come around my camp again with a loaded gun...!

LANCE. Let go of me, don't fucking tell me — gimme back my gun —

RAFE. *(Violently shaking Lance.)* Don't you never ... you hear me? You hear me? You hear me?

LANCE. *(Shocked and too drunk to fight.)* Okay, shit, let go.... *(Rafe hurls him away. Lance staggers, almost falls, stares at Rafe. So does Dylan. Long moment as Rafe fights for control, then:)*

RAFE. This is *my place.* Don't you *never....* Get outa here. *(Lance stares at Rafe, disbelieving, then looks at Dylan, recognizes him. Dylan doesn't know Lance, meets his look, surprised.) Get out!...* And don't come back till I ask you.

LANCE. Fuck you. And fuck your sister too. *(Rafe jumps him — they go down. Rafe savagely pummels Lance. Dylan leaps on them, tries to pull Rafe off.)*

DYLAN. Rafe! Rafe, he's drunk, he didn't mean it, come on, stop now!... *(Dylan wrestles Rafe off Lance — they roll away. Lance doesn't move ... finally stirs and shakily sits up. Dylan goes over and tries to help Lance up. Lance shoves him away, unsteadily gets to his feet, picks up his gun, almost falling over, and looks at Rafe, who is still struggling to control his rage.)*

LANCE. Some fucking friend.

RAFE. Not no more.

LANCE. ... Fine by me. Fucking head case. *(Starts woozily out.)*

RAFE. I've got a gun too, Lance. You come up here again with a loaded gun, I'll shoot you.

LANCE. *(Stops.)* You're alone, asshole. Ask Ruby. You're alone. *(Lance exits. Crossfade as Rafe and Dylan exit and Dad enters with his chair and a can of beer. He wears a light jacket. He sits, drinks beer. To the audience.)*

DAD. Now I'll just say one thing and then I'll shut up. There are some folks in this world, if they wake up in the morning and they can see dollar signs, it's a good day. And if they can't, it ain't. *(Dad drinks. Lights up on Ruby and Dylan, wearing jackets and sitting on a blanket in the woods, wrapped up in each other.)*

RUBY. You can smell the winter coming out here in the woods.

DYLAN. ... Yeah.

DAD. Now you take Rafe and Evan Brooks ... there's a pair to draw to. Them two were at loggerheads, and they were bound to be. 'Cause when it come to dollar signs, them two were day and night.

RUBY. Well, ain't it time? We gotta move before the snow flies.

DYLAN. ... We got it pretty good here.

RUBY. *(Stunned.)* ... What?...

DYLAN. ... Winter is a lousy time to be on the road. We can stay nice and warm right here.... *(Tries to cuddle her.)*

RUBY. Dylan, I ain't gonna sit around for another winter!

DAD. But, you know, at basics, them two were the same. Neither of 'em could sit still, put their feet up, have a drink — leave it for a while. Hell, no. One of 'em was busy doing nothing, and the other one was busy doing nothing yet.

DYLAN. Okay, look, I don't see moving on when we've got a great opportunity right here —

RUBY. Like what!

DYLAN. Evan Brooks. He's got a lot of money — all these properties, investments, he's partners in all kinds of things — your family's land is nothing compared to what he's got. *(Ruby is upset, off-center. Where's this leading them?)*

DAD. Rafe, now ... he was out there every day, sunup to sundown, with them draft horses, training 'em to do the chores like in Granddad's day. He took and bought a sawmill, one of them that's movable, you sit it on a flatbed and bring the sawmill to the logs. I seen him hauling it with his team of horses, right down the two-lane highway that's the onliest main road from here to anywhere, and stuck behind him was a whole long train of trucks and high-wheelers and rice-burners and macaroni-burners and krautmobiles them city folks like to drive up here. And do you think that boy would turn out, let them folks go by? Hell, no! He was holding up the whole parade and he liked it that way! Now, Brooks would do that too. Far as them two are concerned, they *are* the whole parade.

DYLAN. So we've got to wait, Ruby. We've got to play this out.

RUBY. But we don't need his money if we get outa here!

DYLAN. With what? Do you have any money?

RUBY. ... What I've been saving up lately ... a couple hundred dollars.

DYLAN. I don't even have that. *(She stares at him, devastated.)*

DAD. But here's the difference, and you listen to what I'm telling ya. Every day's a good day for Brooks, 'cause all's he sees is dollar signs every blessed day. But Rafe ... you could put them dollar signs in his food, he'd spit 'em out and rinse his mouth out. *(Calls offstage.)* CEELIE, COME ON OUT HERE AND BRING THAT WHISKEY! *(As Ruby and Dylan continue, Mom enters with the whiskey bottle and shot glass, moves slowly toward Dad. Lights dim on them, leaving them in silhouette, as Mom gives Dad the glass and bottle, stands behind his chair.)*

RUBY. ... You tricked me! You never meant to travel with me —

DYLAN. No, I did, I thought that's what we'd do, at first ... but....

RUBY. Have you ever even been to any of those places?

DYLAN. *(Sadly.)* Oh, yeah ... you don't know....

RUBY. That town in Mexico with the old hotel and the birds ... did you make that up?

DYLAN. ... No ... there is a town ... there is an old hotel.... *(Both try to reconnect, language as love-making.)*

RUBY. ... this old hotel in the square, with a marble fountain ...

DYLAN. ... and the birds, flying south in winter ...

RUBY. ... when they come to fly through this little town in Mexico ...

DYLAN. ... the old hotel is in their path ...

RUBY. ... and they fly right in through the open windows ...

DYLAN. ... this stream of birds with beating wings ...

RUBY. ... and out the other side again ... oh, I want to be there! If we go now, maybe we could see them —

DYLAN. *(Pulling her close.)* Ruby, listen, please, please ... I'm so tired of hitch-hiking. It's so much effort, talking to strangers all day long ... letting them think you're anybody they want you to be. I'm sick of starting over ... begging for jobs that turn my stomach ... sleeping anywhere a stranger'll let me have a bed, a floor —

RUBY. A bed ... alone?

DYLAN. … Sometimes. *(Brief pause.)*

RUBY. I would never do that with somebody I didn't love.

DYLAN. *(Simply.)* You don't know what you'll do. *(A moment, then:)* I can't go back to that. I love living here. It's beautiful … it's clean … I feel so happy here, like I'm finally home … like I'm part of the family that built this house and cared for it and filled it for so many years —

RUBY. *(Bewildered.)* But that's my family —

DYLAN. It was. But your family didn't value it. They gave it up. And Brooks — he doesn't give a damn — I'm the one who holds the house together, who works the land — look at my hands, look at the cuts and calluses and bruises, and you can see *I am* this place! We belong here, Ruby. If we just give Brooks what he wants, he'll —

RUBY. "What he wants?" You mean say yes to everything, like you do?

DYLAN. … Not everything.

RUBY. Like when you hitch-hike, Dylan? Is that what you want me to do?

DYLAN. *(Afraid of what he might have meant.)* No! I'm just saying —

RUBY. I won't be beholden to Brooks or nobody! He can ask *me* for favors, I ain't asking him!

DYLAN. Oh, Jesus, Ruby, please don't mess this up for me….

RUBY. *(Attacks him, pounding on him.)* You stop all this! You stop! You stop! *(Dylan grabs her, holds her. She struggles, then starts to cry, lets him hold her. Crossfade D. to silhouette: Ruby and Dylan, Mom and Dad. Spot on Rafe. To the audience.)*

RAFE. When you go inside the gate, they lock the gate behind you. And when you go inside a door, they lock the door behind you. Pretty soon you're locked so far inside, it's like being underground. And you can't get out. *(Brief pause.)* You think about the air a lot. Feels like there ain't enough. Thousands of men inside them walls, and it's all sealed up. Locked windows with bars on 'em, and all them tight-locked doors. And the ceiling's pressing down on you. Feels like it's hard to breathe. *(Brief pause.)* When your shift's over, they let you free for that little while. But the whole time you're outside, sucking in the clean air and looking at the sky, you got this tightness in your chest and this pressure above your eyes like something pressing down on you, 'cause you gotta go back. You don't want to go to sleep, 'cause that'll bring the time closer when you'll walk through them gates again. And you do, you got to. *(Brief pause.)* Every time you hear them locks start to turn behind you, you want to scream out something and hurl them doors open and run. But you can't. You're in there, you're living in there, like the cons. Only difference is, they know when they're getting out. 'Cause you gotta stay in there long enough to buy your land. And ain't no way of knowing yet how long that'll be. *(The silhouettes have slowly faded to black. Lights up on Dad at C., raising a full shot glass.)*

DAD. Here's to all you lovely people. "As good as you are, I'm as bad as I am. And as bad as I am, I'm as good as you are." *(Dad tosses off the shot as Mom, Rafe, Julie, Ruby and Dylan enter, in jackets or sweaters, with beers and a Coke for Rafe and a few lawn chairs, Dad's placed at C. Notes Rafe's Coke can. To Rafe.)* Come on now, I hardly ever see ya, have a real drink, for Chrissakes.

RAFE. I'll stick with this.

MOM. *(To Dad.)* You told me if I had him over, you wouldn't get *at* him —

DAD. *(Mildly.)* Aw, hush up, woman. *(To Rafe.)* Your ma tells me you're working up to the prison now.

RAFE. That's right.

DAD. Well, that's a man's job, I respect that.

RAFE. I'm just doing it 'cause I got to.

DAD. Well, that's what I'm saying.

RAFE. Gotta have a steady job to get a mortgage.

DAD. ... What the hell you doing now?

RAFE. I ain't changed.

DAD. ... Boy, are you telling me you're gonna pay a bloodsucker's interest on land that this family owned free and clear six months ago?

RAFE. If that's what it takes.

DAD. You just ain't gonna face it that that land is lost to you.

RAFE. It ain't till I say it is.

DAD. ... You ... are the orneriest, pigheadedest, dug-in-deepest son of a bitch that I ever heard of.

RAFE. Prob'ly so.

DAD. *(Breaks into a smile.)* Well, good for you, boy! You want it, you go after it!

RAFE. *(Stony.)* That's what I'm doing. *(Mom has been covertly drifting toward Dylan.)*

MOM. Dylan, you like that pie? There's more.

DYLAN. Oh, no, thanks — it was great, though, thanks.

DAD. *(Abruptly, to Dylan.)* Where you from, boy?

DYLAN. ... No place special.

DAD. Where's your kinfolks?

DYLAN. ... Spread around.

DAD. Don't see 'em?

DYLAN. No, sir.

DAD. So you don't call no place home?

DYLAN. ... This is home for now.

RUBY. We're gonna travel. *(Dylan looks at Ruby. They're still fighting over this — why is she bringing it up now?)*

DAD. Oh, you are. Using what for money?

RUBY. You and me gotta talk about that private.

DAD. Oh you say so, do you? *(Slaps his knee.)* Come on over here and sit. *(Everyone is stunned by the implications. Ruby sits on Dad's lap, picks up the bottle and pours him a stiff shot. Mom takes Ruby's seat by Dylan, who is watching Ruby. To Dylan.)* What you got to offer, boy?

DYLAN. ... I'm a hard worker, sir.

DAD. Rafe here is the hardest goddamn worker in the county. What's it got him?

RAFE. I can stand to look in the mirror every morning.

DAD. Aw hell, you ain't even got a mirror. *(To Dylan.)* Rafe here is my boy, and pigheaded as he is, I stand by him because he's mine. But I never made nothing easy for him in his life, no more'n my dad did for me.

DYLAN. I'm not asking for help from you.

DAD. Well, good. Then who is? *(Brooks enters. Everyone is flustered. Ruby jumps up, Dad rises.)* Well, looky here! Come on in, neighbor —

BROOKS. Hello, everybody — didn't know I was interrupting a party — call me Evan, please — I can't stay, I — I'm not much for drinking —

DAD. Ruby, get a beer for Mr. Brooks — or would you have a *real* drink with me?

DAD. Beer ain't drinking, Evan. Had your supper yet? *(Ruby hands Brooks a beer. He smiles at her, takes it and glances at Dad.)*

BROOKS. Uh, well, enough that ... really, I just had an impulse ... I'm driving back to the city in about an hour, and I wondered if Ruby ... if you wouldn't mind if Ruby came along for a visit. *(Dead silence. Everyone looks at Ruby, who tries to seem nonchalant. Mom murmurs in Dylan's ear.)*

MOM. You see how she is?

DAD. *(Speechless for once.)* ... What ... you ... what?

BROOKS. Ruby was telling me a while back that she'd like to see the city. And I have a big place. Guest rooms and all that. Comforts of home, you know. I thought you might feel safer with somebody you know looking after her.

DAD. *(Instantly.)* Oh, no question. *(Beat; trying to assess this.)* Well ... Ruby...? *(Ruby won't look at Dylan. She loves this high drama. Suddenly she smiles at Brooks.)*

RUBY. Why not?

DYLAN. What about your job?

DAD. Oh, we'll take care of that.

BROOKS. Well, fine, then I'll swing by for you in about an hour ... *(Smiles at her, catches himself; to Dad.)* Thanks for the beer. *(To Mom as he goes.)* Bye-bye.

MOM. *(Quietly.)* Bye-bye. *(Brooks goes out. When he's out of earshot, Ruby starts out, passing Dad.)*

RUBY. Well, I better figure out what clothes to take —

DAD. Private talks, eh? I *guess* you've been having some private talks. *(To Dylan.)* You better have another beer, son. Ain't no keeping up with her. *(Dylan bolts offstage. Ruby's scared, but too stubborn to go after him.)*

RUBY. *(To Dad.)* I'm not changing. I'm just making sure.

DAD. Listen. My girl deserves the best. Didn't I always say

so? Just don't get pigheaded like your brother. If you really got a chance ... you're a smart girl. Be smart. *(Ruby looks at Mom.)*

MOM. If I was your age, I'd go after him. And I'd get him, too. *(Dad laughs, enjoying this sexy side of Mom. Ruby looks at Rafe.)*

RAFE. *(Simply.)* He could change everything for me.

RUBY. We don't even know what he wants yet.

DAD. *(Slaps her on the butt.)* Well, go find out, girl! *(Ruby laughs, trying for bravado, exits. Dad looks at Mom, who avoids his look and exits. Dad follows, leaving Rafe with Julie.)*

JULIE. She's gonna get it all, ain't she? I'd like to kill her.

RAFE. Easy now.

JULIE. You're crazy if you think she'll help you.

RAFE. Maybe ... maybe not. *(Rafe and Julie exit. Crossfade to the sunny Carroll kitchen. Mom sits on a chair beside a laundry basket, folding laundry on her lap. Dylan enters. He's showing the strain since Ruby left with Brooks.)*

DYLAN. Hi, Mrs. Carroll — Ceelie. *(Shaken, Mom can't speak.)* Sorry to bother you ... I just, you know, came by to see if —

MOM. *(Rises, overlapping.)* You ain't bothering ... come on in, come in.

DYLAN. Oh, thanks. I just was wondering if Ruby's back yet —

MOM. You want to sit down? *(Puts the folded laundry in the basket.)*

DYLAN. ... Oh ... well, that's okay....

MOM. You look tired. Sit down.

DYLAN. *(Sits.)* ... I guess I kind of....

MOM. Look like you need a good night's sleep.

DYLAN. ... Yeah, I'm not....

MOM. And a good meal. What you been eating over there?

DYLAN. ... Oh, you know....

MOM. I'll fix you a plate. *(Starts out.)*

DYLAN. Oh no, don't bother —

MOM. It won't take a minute. We got a microwave. I'll fix you something, then we'll talk — *(Starts out again.)*

DYLAN. No! I mean, it's really nice of you but I ... I've gotta get back to work....

MOM. You work too hard. Time he gets back, Brooks won't even notice all you done.

DYLAN. Did Ruby call? Do you know when they're getting back?

MOM. No. She'll do how she wants. And we all gotta step in line.

DYLAN. *(Beat.)* Don't you like her?

MOM. ... She's mine. I got a pride in her. But she always done like that. *(Cautiously lays her hand on his back, "comforting" him. Quietly:)* She done it with her father, with every man she come upon. And when I seen her looking at you on the road, first day you was up this way, I knew what she'd do. She'd make you follow in her path. And she'd be careless of you. *(Pause.)*

DYLAN. *(Very upset, rises.)* I gotta go. Could you let me know if she calls?

MOM. *(Gently.)* Sure. But she won't. That ain't Ruby.

DYLAN. *(Not knowing what else to say.)* ... Well ... thanks.... *(He exits. Mom watches him with longing. Crossfade to Rafe's campsite, night. It's cold. Rafe and Julie sit by the fire on a sleeping bag. Rafe's rifle is nearby, broken open for safety. Rafe is coaxing Julie to make love.)*

JULIE. Rafe ...

RAFE. Ssshhh ... *(He kisses her. She breaks it.)*

JULIE. It's cold. Are you gonna get yourself a real place to live or not? We can't keep doing like this, and you got a good job now —

RAFE. I'm gonna stay right here as long as I can. It's rugged. But the more money I save, the quicker I can buy that land.

JULIE. The meadow.

RAFE. Yeah. And after that, maybe the long field —

JULIE. "After that?" He wants a hundred thousand for that pukey little meadow! How much is he gonna want for the long field?

RAFE. I can't worry about that yet —

JULIE. For a hundred thousand dollars, you can buy a working farm, right here in this county, with a house and a barn and —

RAFE. I don't want them farms. This is my land. I'm meant to have it, Julie. You gotta back me up on this. We'll ... we'll work things out about *us*....

JULIE. I give up, Rafe.

RAFE. ... Don't give up....

JULIE. I am. Don't come around. I mean it.

RAFE. *(Beat.)* Up to you. I'll miss you. *(Julie slaps him, hard. He stares, amazed, then grabs her arm, anger flying up.)* Don't you never do that again.

JULIE. No, I won't. I won't care enough. *(She exits. Slowly, Rafe sits, stares at the fire. Silence. Then noises are heard in the brush.)*

RAFE. *(Rises.)* Julie? *(Waits. No reply.)* JULIE, ANSWER IF THAT'S YOU!... WHO'S OUT THERE? *(No reply; grabs his gun, fires a warning shot.)*

DYLAN. *(Offstage.)* HEY, IT'S DYLAN!

RAFE. *(Lowers the gun.)* COME AHEAD! *(Dylan enters, carrying a much-used duffel bag. He's in a shaky state, and the shot didn't help. He stops, looks at Rafe and the gun.)* I'm careful now, is all. *(Dylan nods, pulling himself together. Rafe breaks open the gun. Then:)* Ruby back?

DYLAN. ... No ... no ... *(Long beat; with an effort.)* I haven't heard from her.

RAFE. ... Huh. *(Beat.)* Want a Coke?

DYLAN. *(Long beat.)* Listen. *(Longer beat.)* I found something. *(Dylan squats, opens the duffel bag, takes out a cardboard box. Rafe lays the gun down. Dylan holds the box for a beat, then holds it out to Rafe. Rafe looks at Dylan, takes the box, squats, sets the box down carefully. He opens it gently, looks in for a long moment. He looks at Dylan. Then he lifts out some long bones, holds them up in the firelight.)* I was digging. Planting trees. Between the farmhouse and the road.

RAFE. *(Examining the bones.)* Don't look like any animal bones I've ever seen. You found 'em by the farmhouse?

DYLAN. *(Nods.)* It's your family's land. I thought....

RAFE. You brung 'em to me. That was right. *(Rafe puts the*

bones gently back in the box, and closes it, shaken but trying not to show it.) No way of telling who it is or how they got there.
DYLAN. No way *we* can tell.
RAFE. ... I'll bury 'em up here. *(Dylan nods. Rafe holds his gaze, then:)* 'Preciate it. *(They both rise.)*
DYLAN. I need help from you.
RAFE. You got a right now. But if it's Ruby, I can't side with you.
DYLAN. Brooks is never gonna give you what you want!
RAFE. He don't have to give it to me, I'm earning it —
DYLAN. He doesn't care! About *anybody!* Not even Ruby.
RAFE. We don't know that yet. *(Beat; gently.)* You don't gotta get caught in this. I'd move on if I was you.
DYLAN. I can't ... I can't move on. *(Rafe looks at him with empathy. But he makes a helpless gesture like his mother's.)*
RAFE. I'll go get the spade. *(Rafe exits. Dylan watches; then in a wild impulse, he grabs Rafe's gun and runs out. Crossfade to the Carrolls' yard. Mom stands in the darkness, gazing toward the farmhouse, thinking of Dylan. Dad enters from the shadows, puts his arms around her. He's a little drunk.)*
DAD. ... Ceelie ... what are you doing out here in the dark? Come on to bed, girl.
MOM. ... I'll sit up a while.
DAD. Aw hell, why should them kids have all the fun? *(Nuzzling her.)* "Ceelie, put that flashlight down...."
MOM. You're too drunk, Marlin. Don't waste my time.
DAD. *(Long beat; lets go of her.)* You sure got dried up fast. *(He slowly exits. Mom continues gazing out. Crossfade to the farmhouse porch. Darkness. Dylan has Rafe's gun, sits motionless. After a beat, Rafe enters cautiously. He can't see Dylan in the dark, but senses his presence. He stops, squats, ready to flatten himself if Dylan fires.)*
RAFE. *(Gently.)* Dylan? *(Dylan jumps. The gun jumps but doesn't fire. Bent low, Rafe keeps moving as he speaks.)* Okay, now ... I come to get my gun. *(Rafe stops, flattens himself on the ground. He and Dylan are still. Then:)* I don't know what you plan to do with it. *(Crouches, moving as he speaks.)* But ain't no harm done yet. You can just give it back to me. *(Rafe flattens himself*

again. No response.) Come on, let's talk about it. *(No response. Rafe moves again, flattens. Faint light up on Mom behind the screen, only a few feet from Dylan, hiding inside the farmhouse. Scared, very still, she listens.)* Dylan, now you know I can't let you do like this. *(Waits. No answer. Moves again.)* Okay, I'm gonna hafta go get help. I don't wanta do that. But I can't let you have that gun. *(Beat; Dylan raises the gun, points it toward Rafe. Rafe rises, bent low, moves in a crooked route toward offstage. Dylan remains poised to shoot, following the faint sounds Rafe makes, till Rafe is gone. Then Mom speaks from her hiding place.)*

MOM. I'm here. *(Dylan swings the gun in her direction, then lowers it, jumps up, very shaken.)*

DYLAN. Ruby?

MOM. *(Comes onto the porch.)* Ceelie. I'm here.

DYLAN. Is Ruby back?

MOM. Dylan, she's with *him.* *(Shattered, Dylan just stands there. A still moment; then Mom moves to him, touches his face delicately. Desperate for contact and tenderness, he lets it happen. She's terrified but can't stop — she kisses him, touches him. Still clutching the gun, Dylan feels himself sinking, helpless.)*

DYLAN. ... I can't do that anymore. Please ... go away ... go home....

MOM. *(Passion rising.)* No, listen ... I got money hid from him ... I take it from his pockets when he's drunk ... I never knew what I was gonna do with it ... but I just had to hide it and count it up ... you can have it....

DYLAN. That's not what I want.

MOM. I'll get Ruby back for you. *(Dylan is torn, bewildered: can she really do that?)*

DYLAN. ... You ... you better get outa here ... I don't know what's gonna happen....

MOM. I know how to do with her ... make her think she's losing something ... she'll come running back.... *(Mom kisses Dylan. He gives in, then pulls away, putting the gun between them.)*

DYLAN. Get outa here, I told you!

MOM. But I'll help you, I'll do anything you —

DYLAN. Get away from me!

MOM. Oh, please, please —

DYLAN. Please don't make me hurt you —

MOM. I gotta have *something!*

DYLAN. *(Points the shaking rifle at her.) Get out! Get out! (Mom exits. Crossfade to the Carrolls' yard. Ruby and Brooks walk slowly toward the Carroll house. Brooks carries Ruby's suitcase. Ruby wears a new, moderately expensive jacket.)*

RUBY. I love this jacket.

BROOKS. My pleasure. And we didn't go overboard, so hopefully it won't make your parents nervous.

RUBY. They won't care. I like your car, too.

BROOKS. You do, huh? Not too many of those in your neck of the woods.... Looks like your folks are out.

RUBY. Them? They're asleep ... I had a real good time.

BROOKS. Well, good. We'll do it again, if you're interested.

RUBY. Oh, I could live like that.

BROOKS. *(Amused.)* Takes money.

RUBY. You've got that part.

BROOKS. *(Laughs, but he's interested.)* Is this a proposal? *(Ruby gives a little ambiguous smile. Brooks stops walking, trying to read her. She stops too, but gives nothing away.)* You'd be shocked if I took you up on it.

RUBY. Why?

BROOKS. ... Well, you're seventeen —

RUBY. Eighteen. And you're not that much older.

BROOKS. ... Well ... there *is* a gap. Your life and mine combined ... that's quite an image. I'd have to send you to college, for starters.... But you're something, Ruby. I've got to be careful not to spend too much time around you. *(Beat; he gives in, moves to kiss her.)*

RUBY. I wouldn't give up Dylan for all your money.

BROOKS. *(Freezes, pulls back.)* ... Really. I didn't see you as a romantic, Ruby. And I can't imagine Dylan will be able to keep you in the style you aspire to. Even with a second income from McDonald's.

RUBY. We're leaving anyway.

BROOKS. He hasn't told me.

RUBY. I just did.

BROOKS. *(Beat.)* I hurt your feelings, didn't I? I'm sorry, that was stupid of me —

RUBY. That's not why. *(Takes her suitcase.)* It was fun. Thanks. *(She kisses him, long enough to let him know what he'll be missing, and exits. He watches her. Crossfade to the farmhouse. Rafe and Dad approach very cautiously in the dark, with rifles.)*

DAD. *(Softly.)* Think he's waiting there for Ruby and Brooks?

RAFE. *(Softly.)* I dunno. Maybe not, maybe he won't hurt nobody —

DAD. We gotta make sure of that.

RAFE. You talk to him. Maybe he'll give the gun to you —

DAD. Maybe he'll shoot me too. Don't pull back now. I ain't gonna shoot unless I got to, but I need you to follow my lead here. Will you do that?

RAFE. Yeah.

DAD. That's why you came and got me, ain't it? *(Rafe takes this as a deep cut. Softly, they walk forward a few feet. Then:)* Stop here. Now stay pretty close. We don't want to fan out too much, might shoot each other.

RAFE. ... Right.

DAD. Wisht it wasn't so goddamn dark. *(Turns head to listen.)* Car coming. Might be them. *(Dad crouches, gun ready. Rafe follows his lead. Faint light maintains on Rafe and Dad. Lights up on Dylan, behind the screen door. Sounds of car arriving. Dylan listens, rifle held at his side. Headlights sweep across the porch, go out. Car sounds out. Dylan waits with every nerve. Faint light up on Ruby in another area, walking through the meadow in the dark. She's coming to Dylan but taking her time, feeling very happy and powerful, and humming the melody of "Mill o' Tifty's Annie." She looks up at the stars, stretches up as if to touch them, and turns slowly, starting to dance. Humming continues till indicated. Dylan speaks aloud the words he's been going over and over in his head for days.)*

DYLAN. Mr. Brooks ... I just want to ask you respectfully ... see, Ruby and I are ... Ruby means more to me, and we ... we don't have any other place to go ... and we belong here, Mr. Brooks.... *(Brooks enters, calls from darkness.)*

BROOKS. HEY, DYLAN! PUT THE PORCH LIGHT ON! *(Ruby's humming is the only sound. Behind the screen door, Dylan hesitates, then flicks an unseen switch. A pool of light falls on the porch. Dylan is clearly seen behind the door.)*

DAD. *(Positioned to fire, mutters.)* There's his mistake, right there. You ready?

RAFE. Maybe he's just got that gun because he's scared.

DAD. Him or you? *(Trembling, Rafe raises his gun, stands ready. Brooks, with his briefcase, enters the porch. He steps into the light, throws a hand up to shield his eyes from the sudden glare.)*

DYLAN. Mr. Brooks ... where's Ruby?

BROOKS. *(Trying to be amused.)* Well, you won, Dylan.

DYLAN. ... What? *(Ruby hums and dances as Dylan opens the screen door and enters the porch, the rifle dangling in his hand.)* What did you say?

BROOKS. What's with the gun? *(As if he'd forgotten it, Dylan makes a dazed, explaining gesture that sweeps the rifle upward. Convulsively, Rafe fires. Dylan jerks backward and falls as Rafe lets out a shocked cry and drops his gun.)*

DAD. *Goddamnit, you fired too soon! (Blackout on all but Ruby, who has heard the shot, the cries. She stops, frightened, then cries out.)*

RUBY. *Dylan!! (She starts to run. Blackout.)*

DAD'S VOICE. Well, Christ ... for good or ill ... you got him, son. *(Country instrumental music picks up the song. As it fades, lights up on Dad and Rafe in one area, and Ruby and Mom in another area. Ruby lies in a heap on the floor, face in her arms. Mom sits beside her, motionless, knowing that she must comfort her but too desolate to do it. In the other area, Rafe, in shock, sits on a kitchen chair. Dad has the shot glass and bottle, pours a hefty shot and downs it. Spot on Brooks. To the audience.)*

BROOKS. I wanted to call the troopers. To his credit, so did Rafe. But his father was convinced that to keep Rafe out of prison, we had to handle it ourselves. And Rafe had saved my life ... or meant to, anyway ... so I left them to it. I think they must have buried him where he had been planting trees ... not far from the house.... Well, obviously, after that I couldn't even go there. So I sold the property. I thought Rafe would want to buy the meadow, and I would have felt compelled to sell it to him ... probably ... but I never heard from him. Or Ruby either.... Strange people. *(Lights down on Brooks.)*

DAD. *(To Rafe.)* Oh, I know I had a part in it. And I gotta carry that. And I will. I do. But you know, more than that, what I think is, that boy of Ruby's was disturbed ... twisted up inside, like a tree that's windshook. Sometimes you take and cut a hemlock down that looks beautiful, tall and straight and fine. But when you cut it open, it just falls apart. 'Cause it's been so twisted and wrenched around by these winds up here in these mountains that the grain can't hold together. The other trees can take it, but a windshook tree ... you take and cut it open, and it crumbles in your hands ... *(Dad pours another shot, offers it to Rafe, who doesn't even see it. Dad waits a beat, drinks it himself. Crossfade slowly down on Ruby and Mom, up on Darlene in another area.)*

DARLENE. I think I'm the only outside one who knows. Well, Ruby had to have someone to talk to ... acting all crazy like she was ... I guess she knew I'd understand how it coulda happened, 'cause Dale and me ... I hate to think it, 'specially 'cause of Ashley, but *we* could end up some way like that. Shit happens.... But then Ruby's dad give her some money and she left. Taking the bus across the country, going to Mexico. She sent me a postcard from some little town out west where they got folks dress up like cowboys and Indians and act out scenes, you know. That was the picture on the postcard. I woulda like to seen that show. But after that, nobody heard nothing ... not even her mom and dad.... And Rafe, I woulda thought he'd go away too, but he just kept going. Got a good promotion at the prison. Sold off them big old horses and rented that apartment above the hardware store, you know. Julie fixed it up real nice ... come summer, they got married. *(Dad pours a third shot, holds it out to Rafe. Rafe doesn't move. Dad waits.)* But pretty soon, every week end, Rafe'd be back up there at his campsite on that mountainside ... trying to clear that land that was mostly rocks and trees. Wanted to build a cabin, somewheres around there where his granddad's cabin used to be. *(Lights down on Darlene. Beat; not looking at his father, Rafe takes and drinks the shot.)*

END OF PLAY

PROPERTY LIST

Trowel (MOM)
Dirt-caked garden gloves (RUBY)
Backpack (DYLAN)
Bedroll (DYLAN)
2 yellow bow corsages (JULIE, MOM)
Cheap folding chair (RUBY, DAD)
Small yellow ribbon (JULIE)
Six-pack of cheap beer
Can of Coke (MOM)
Fifth of whiskey (RUBY, MOM, DAD)
Shot glass (RUBY, MOM, DAD)
Wheelbarrow with fireplace-size logs (DYLAN)
Shoulder bag with McDonald's cap and uniform (RUBY)
Paper grocery bag with McDonald's uniform (DARLENE)
Purse (DARLENE)
Cigarettes and lighter or matches (DARLENE)
Ponytail clip (DARLENE)
Old truck carburetor (RAFE)
Small wrenches (RAFE)
Screwdrivers (RAFE)
Sack lunch (DAD)
Thermos of coffee (DAD)
Spade (DYLAN)
Flashlight (RAFE)
Pack (RAFE)
Tote bag (JULIE) with:
- paper plates
- matching napkins
- grapes
- cheese knife
- French crackers
- 2 slabs of cheese

Bottle of Coke (RAFE)
Old bucket of firewood (RAFE)
Briefcase (BROOKS)

Deli sandwich in a paper sack (BROOKS)
3 imported beers (BROOKS)
Wallet fat with money and credit cards (BROOKS)
Business cards (BROOKS)
Bowl of peaches (MOM, JULIE)
Two small sharp knives (MOM, JULIE)
Mug of coffee (BROOKS)
Beer can in a sack (LANCE)
Hunting rifles (RAFE, LANCE)
Can of beer (DAD)
Blanket (RUBY, DYLAN)
Lawn chairs (RAFE)
Cokes (RAFE)
Beers (MOM, JULIE, RUBY, DYLAN)
Unfolded laundry in a basket (MOM)
Duffel bag (DYLAN)
Cardboard box of bones (DYLAN)
Suitcase (BROOKS)
2 rifles (RAFE, DAD)

SOUND EFFECTS

Rifle shot
Car arriving

NEW PLAYS

• **TAKING SIDES by Ronald Harwood.** Based on the true story of one of the world's greatest conductors whose wartime decision to remain in Germany brought him under the scrutiny of a U.S. Army determined to prove him a Nazi. *"A brave, wise and deeply moving play delineating the confrontation between culture, and power, between art and politics, between irresponsible freedom and responsible compromise." --London Sunday Times.* [4M, 3W] ISBN: 0-8222-1566-7

• **MISSING/KISSING by John Patrick Shanley.** Two biting short comedies, MISSING MARISA and KISSING CHRISTINE, by one of America's foremost dramatists and the Academy Award winning author of *Moonstruck*. *" ... Shanley has an unusual talent for situations ... and a sure gift for a kind of inner dialogue in which people talk their hearts as well as their minds...." --N.Y. Post.* MISSING MARISA [2M], KISSING CHRISTINE [1M, 2W] ISBN: 0-8222-1590-X

• **THE SISTERS ROSENSWEIG by Wendy Wasserstein, Pulitzer Prize-winning author of *The Heidi Chronicles*.** Winner of the 1993 Outer Critics Circle Award for Best Broadway Play. A captivating portrait of three disparate sisters reuniting after a lengthy separation on the eldest's 50th birthday. *"The laughter is all but continuous." --New Yorker. "Funny. Observant. A play with wit as well as acumen.... In dealing with social and cultural paradoxes, Ms. Wasserstein is, as always, the most astute of commentators." --N.Y. Times.* [4M, 4W] ISBN: 0-8222-1348-6

• **MASTER CLASS by Terrence McNally. Winner of the 1996 Tony Award for Best Play.** Only a year after winning the Tony Award for *Love! Valour! Compassion!*, Terrence McNally scores again with the most celebrated play of the year, an unforgettable portrait of Maria Callas, our century's greatest opera diva. *"One of the white-hot moments of contemporary theatre. A total triumph." --N.Y. Post. "Blazingly theatrical." -- USA Today.* [3M, 3W] ISBN: 0-8222-1521-7

• **DEALER'S CHOICE by Patrick Marber.** A weekly poker game pits a son addicted to gambling against his own father, who also has a problem but won't admit it. *"... make tracks to DEALER'S CHOICE, Patrick Marber's wonderfully masculine, razor-sharp dissection of poker-as-life.... It's a play that comes out swinging and never lets up -- a witty, wisecracking drama that relentlessly probes the tortured souls of its six very distinctive ... characters. CHOICE is a cutthroat pleasure that you won't want to miss." --Time Out (New York).* [6M] ISBN: 0-8222-1616-7

• **RIFF RAFF by Laurence Fishburne.** RIFF RAFF marks the playwriting debut of one of Hollywood's most exciting and versatile actors. *"Mr. Fishburne is surprisingly and effectively understated, with scalding bubbles of anxiety breaking through the surface of a numbed calm." --N.Y. Times. "Fishburne has a talent and a quality...[he] possesses one of the vital requirements of a playwright -- a good ear for the things people say and the way they say them." --N.Y. Post.* [3M] ISBN: 0-8222-1545-4